LETTERS
TO A
YOUNG ARTIST

LETTERS TO A YOUNG ARTIST

from

Gregory Amenoff, Jo Baer,
John Baldessari, Xu Bing,
Jimmie Durham, Joseph Grigely,
Guerrilla Girls, Cai Guo-Qiang,
Joan Jonas, Alex Katz,
John McCracken, Kerry James Marshall,
Elizabeth Murray,
Thomas Nozkowski, Yoko Ono,
Howardena Pindell, Adrian Piper,
William Pope.L, Yvonne Rainer,
Stephen Shore, Jessica Stockholder,
Mierle Laderman Ukeles, Lawrence Weiner

An Art on Paper Book
Darte Publishing, New York

4

In the summer of 2005, *Art on Paper* magazine published a special issue titled "Letters to a Young Artist." Inspired by Rainer Maria Rilke's "Letters to a Young Poet," it included a collection of twelve letters by established artists written in response to a letter from a fictional "young artist."

This book, which includes twenty-three letters, expands on this idea and provides an even greater range of opinions and words of wisdom, often surprising, by many of today's most revered artists. We have read these letters many times and they continue to touch our hearts, incite our curiosity, and enrich our understanding of both the greater art world and the inner workings of a creative mind. And like Rilke's, the advice they contain transcends the discipline of art: these are life lessons.

We are publishing this book in a small, pocket-size format to encourage you to carry it around with you - referring to it for inspiration when necessary - and to pass it on to friends. Cai Guo-Qiang, who grew up in China, jokingly referred to it as the "little green book," likening it, in format at least, to Mao's little red book.

One last note: the original letter from the young artist is not published here. As you read on, however, you will see recurring patterns of thought that will help you to reconstruct it in your own way.

Peter Nesbett, Shelly Bancroft, Sarah Andress

A NOTE TO THE READER FROM THE YOUNG ARTIST

Eighteen months ago, I graduated from art school and moved to New York City from the West Coast. I was excited about the prospect of living and making art in what many say is still the heart of the contemporary art world. The museums. The galleries and nonprofit spaces. The music clubs. A community of peers. I remember the exhilaration I felt when I first arrived, sleeping on a friend's couch while I looked for my first apartment.

That seems like a long time ago. Since then I've been overwhelmed by the challenges of trying to make ends meet. When I'm not at my job – where I spend most of my time – I'm either out looking at exhibitions or I'm holed up in my room trying to make my art. In short, I've been spending a lot of time alone in a city teaming with people. The few friends I have made are artists, many of whom are already showing and selling their work. Not me, although I've had the chance. Call me a purist, but I think it is important for artists to develop a true sense of themselves before showing their work, so as not to be tempted or tainted by commercial ambition. I struggle with many aspects of the art business, which at the moment appears to be ruled by fashion and greed.

Feeling the need to connect with someone who has already lived the life I am living, I decided to write a letter to an established artist whose work I deeply admire. Just the process of writing the letter was therapeutic, and I wasn't expecting I'd actually receive a response. But several weeks later, I did. I was shocked. Reading it, I felt buoyed, energized, and heartened by the engagement.

I began writing to other artists, one by one, selecting those who seem to have approached their careers with passion and integrity. Each response emboldened me to write again and over time I accumulated almost two dozen letters from artists in the United States and abroad. The letters have prompted me to take a good look in the mirror, to question my fears, ambitions, prejudices, and assumptions.

I share the letters with you here exactly as I received them, with the hope that they may be of as much value for you as they have been for me.

Dear Young Artist,

I did not answer your letter sooner, first because I am very busy and second because the honest and specific questions in your letter cannot be answered simply, in a few words. The situation of each person who engages in art is unique and bears its own conditions. In addition, even those artists who have already succeeded when asked why others have not, have trouble answering the question despite their natural talents.

One can see from your letter that you are a person who has courage when it comes to your future and your artistic responsibilities. This is not something that everyone possesses; but it is the first condition of being a successful, outstanding artist. You should recognize this. I have always thought that to be an artist, the first thing you must do is clarify what art is and what its principles are. Specifically speaking, you must identify what an artist does in this world and what relationship exists between yourself, society, and culture. And even more specifically, you must determine your particular commutative relationship with society. If you want to be a person who can survive on your art, you must clarify what can be exchanged with society before society will repay you. I sometimes think: I have a house in which to live, a studio in which to work and food to eat – what has been exchanged? Museums and collectors are willing to buy my work for a high price, what have they purchased? The artwork itself is a mere lump of materials; is it worth that much? Does value derive from meticulously cultivated skill? Many artists work more meticulously than I do. Rather, that part of the work with value presents society with a valuable way of thinking and is associated with a new form of artistic expression. As this "new mode" is something that people need, it can become marketable; only then can it constitute a conversion key. The discovery of this new mode springs from talent, a sensitivity to one's time, and an above-average recognition of the current culture and environment. In this way, it restructures the methodologies of old art. Consequently, a good artist is a thinking person, and is adept at translating thoughts into the language of art.

From your letter it is clear that your goals are lofty. At the same time, you are not an artist looking to quickly achieve market results. This is the right way of thinking. Of course, any "value" will be transformed into a commodity and it will ultimately be sold. A street artist might sell one piece every ten minutes; an artist in a gift shop might sell one piece every day; and an artist in a commercial gallery might sell one piece a month. Some people sell a piece as soon as it is finished, others sell only one idea for their entire lives. It all depends on what kind of artist you prefer to be.

Some of the principles I have discussed above are a little broad and do not address the problems you are facing. Below I will bring up some specific examples from my experience, which you might find helpful.

Every person who has studied art wants to become a major artist, but every person's conditions are different. This includes knowledge, artistic sensibility, financial and family background, etc. Everyone has strengths and limitations. Those who know how to work also understand that whatever limitations they meet can be transformed into things that are useful to them. Using a limitation well transforms it into a strength. In China I received a very conservative art education, and I didn't come to America to participate in Western contemporary art until I was thirty-five years old. You and the majority of young artists in America have received an open contemporary art education early in your life. In terms of your linguistic and cultural adaptations, it's easier for you to meld into New York's contemporary art scene. Compared to you, I was not naturally predisposed, but from this "inadequacy" I could extract something to utilize that others have not. Due to my socialist art-education background, I probably view contemporary art from a distinct perspective, which also stems from living in a new cultural environment and confronting language barriers. I am particularly sensitive to language, words, and misreading. My art expresses characteristics that others' art does not.

My viewpoint is that wherever you live, you will face that place's problems. If you have problems then you have art. Your plight and your problems are actually the source of your artistic creation. The majority of young artists who come to New York to develop their careers are eager to enter the mainstream. But, like you, they have to spend time working other jobs to support their costs of living here. It may seem like you are wasting time that could be used for creating art, but you needn't actually worry about this too much. As long as you are a true artist every field that you are engaged in outside of art circles – living and working – will produce treasure, which sooner or later will be used in the creation of your art. It is not important to plunge headlong into this mainstream system. Instead, find a suitable position and relationship to it. But you should know that you must bring something new to this system – something that is not already there – for the system to have a reason to accept you. And it should be something that cannot be found in the system itself. Only if this thing is from some other realm or from the boundary between two regions will it be possible for you to succeed. Today's art has become, on the surface, rich and varied, but in terms of methodology it has also become more and more narrow. Too many artists know how to make "standard" contemporary art. The system really doesn't need any more of this kind of artist.

Just work, and don't worry whether your talent will be discovered. With the speed and ease of communication today, tragedies like those of van

Gogh's time basically do not exist. Museums and curators are the same as artists: They are anxious that no interesting work will come out. So long as you can bring forth something good, museum curators will come to snatch it away for exhibition.

I wish you success,

Xu Bing
New York

Dear Young Artist,

Thanks for the lucid note. I am envious of your age and also your handwriting . . . nothing I can do about the former or the latter, hence the typed response. Rather than frame my reply to you in poetic terms, I have constructed a list of things you might want to remember as you continue on your chosen path in visual art. As you read them, imagine me yelling them at you with urgency!

First and foremost you must remember that ARTISTS DRIVE THE BUS. It is an easy thing to forget. We sometimes feel we are at the bottom of the heap (artist as victim). But for an artist in his/her studio, working in relative isolation and producing objects from the imagination, there is nothing of what we call the art world – no critics, no curators, no art historians or art history departments, no museums, no art books or art libraries, no magazines, no auction houses, and, finally, no galleries. The entire enterprise is built on one central event: the creative act in the studio. I mean no arrogance here, but it is simply true. I don't know whether we are the plankton or the whale, but we are indispensable.

That said, LET YOUR STUDIO BE YOUR SANCTUARY. Have no illusions . . . the art business, despite the pretension that surrounds "cultural products," has more in common with other businesses than it does with art. When your work leaves your studio and moves into the world, its character changes. One doesn't need to consult a Marxist to understand that art is a luxury commodity. You learn to live with this fact (and find ways of justifying it), but in the studio things are different. Within that space you create and take chances, destroy, and create again. If the marketplace finds its way (spiritually) into that studio you have abdicated your essential power. Keep your studio clear from concerns of the marketplace. You might have to dance with the wolves but you can still keep them near the door.

Speaking of work in the studio – DON'T BE AFRAID TO DO DUMB THINGS IN THE STUDIO. Artists can't get anywhere beyond the familiar and the prevalidated without risking being ridiculous. We would not have Guston's late work had he not willingly risked "dumbness."

A quick one – KEEP AWAY FROM ART FAIRS. Instead, visit a museum and spend time in a wing housing art from centuries past. You will be rejuvenated, not demoralized.

SUPPORT YOUR FELLOW ARTISTS AS THEY SUPPORT YOU. Your best community is your peer group of fellow artists. Openings are wonderful events, when artists come together to celebrate one another. Sure, they are great places to extend your network, but they are primarily events to extend community beyond the studio. We live in a country where culture is marginalized . . . all the more reason we should support our own efforts. Artists like Joan Mitchell, Adolph Gottlieb, Robert Mapplethorpe, and Andy Warhol all set up foundations to help artists in perpetuity. What a testament to their generosity!

READ BIOGRAPHIES OF ARTISTS. The lives of other artists can illuminate various ways to approach your own life as an artist, and those narratives can also help you see beyond the conditions of our particular time.

It's great to have lots of shows and sell lots of work but that alone will not fulfill you. To paraphrase the late, wise painter Harvey Quaytman – A LIFE IN ART IS A LONG RACE NOT A SHORT SPRINT. Can you imagine a rich shape for your creative life beyond the standard measures of fame and financial success? If you begin to answer that question when you are young, you will have a leg up when you find yourself in your mid and late career.

All the best,

Gregory Amenoff
New York

22.

Dear Young Artist:

I became a painter because I went to a school that was in a great museum. Walking to class, I started to see the paintings, quietly waiting to be seen. They penetrated and I realized I wanted to make paintings as intense and moving as those on the wall. I had wanted to be a commercial artist. Instead, I started trying to paint. Here are some suggestions as you begin your career:

Stay in touch with your original motivation to become an artist — and be aware that it is always a process of becoming. You have to stay light on your feet. It is about change and transformation. You are the boss of that but you don't have total control. Good to give into that. Making art requires a lot of isolation, but I realized over time that I also wanted a whole life, that I could still do my work and have a partner and a family. So have a life. Art making fits in well.

Showing your work — eventually selling work — is not evil, and it is a natural process. You are not selling your soul, you are earning a living, and you don't have to do anything you feel is wrong. If you make some money and get attention for what you have done, your friends may be envious. Forgive them — you'll have those feelings, too. Only human.

The art world seems to conjure up a lot of nonsense right now and seems to be only about trends, money, and fame. Try to stay focused and centered in what you want in your work, keeping in mind that your art is about describing your spirit and your life force makes the work better.

Good luck. You are already succeeding just by attempting.

Elizabeth Murray
New York

Young artist to be,

You *should* have grandiose ideas about your future success. No one with small ambitions and vague goals ever amounted to much in this game.

Since childhood, I dreamt of being counted among the great artists whose work inspires young doodlers to say: "That's what I want to do . . . I want to make something like that!" I wanted my work to be in museum collections, I didn't want to just go there to see the work of others. I only wish my art school education had been rigorous enough to prepare the way. When I left school, I felt, as you seem to, at the mercy of mysterious authorities I did not know, and forces beyond my control. I had done some exercises, and made a few things, but never felt I really learned anything. A hope and a prayer was all I really had to go on. There was nothing to look forward to, nothing to work toward. I was told, "There's nothing you can do. Shut up and do your work . . . they'll let you know if you make the grade." That arrangement is unreliable, and totally unacceptable. Never surrender your dream to chance, alone.

Needless to say, I was angry and bitter after school. I felt there were important and concrete lessons to learn, but few teachers seemed willing or able to pass the information on. At this point, I understand a thing or two. What I've learned since school gives me many reasons to be very particular about with whom I share this knowledge. Your letter provides no specific information about your identity. I have no idea who you are. The appeal seems genuine enough, though, so despite some reservations, I'll take a chance this once.

You are barely one year out of art school, so what you might be experiencing are symptoms of withdrawal, not unlike those associated with mind-altering drugs. You've been on a bad trip, and it's going to take a little while to connect with reality. There are some things you can do, a few techniques that have worked for me, to minimize the confusion and trauma.

Art schools are sort of like Crack dens. While inside, the environment feels cozy, everything there seems remarkable because you're all smoking from the same pipe. In the heady, hazy fog of dialogue and critique, the smallest achievements are amplified. You begin to believe that things you make or do have value simply because you made or did them. Your friends are all supportive, they like your stuff. "It is all very interesting, a nice piece." Be wary of this incessant chatter. In the sober world, the world outside, nobody really cares. Here, you have to win attention, and the span allotted for recognition and celebrity is short and narrow, indeed. Nevertheless, you did inhale lots of bullshit, and now it's time to blow it out and rehabilitate.

Recognizing the delusions is the first step toward recovery, and, more likely than not, a successful career as an artist.

Nobody with an undersized ego gets into this game.

Everything is not OK!

Always choose subjects that matter to you.

The opponent is subjectivity.

Artists are not magicians or shamans, prophets or seers. We make stuff, and the devices we use to "transfigure the commonplace" are recognizable. Isolate, re-contextualize, shift scale, shift material, invert, etc. The special status of art has more to do with its relationship to power and money than with any inherent attribute.

Every day in the studio is another step toward being all that you can be. Marcel Duchamp thought of the studio as a "laboratory." Embrace this concept. Offset and solve concrete problems. Inspiration is generated by work.

Synthesize, Synthesize, Synthesize. Force relationships between forms that may seem incompatible. If they fuse, maybe you've found something fresh. This procedure should be carried out with the methodical precision of a chemical engineer.

Attend to the function of your work, its performance within a certain genre, instead of its meaning. It is not the subject matter, per se, it's the treatment that matters.

Name your ambition. One has to be very clear about what it is that "Artists" do. Then ask, what kind of "Artist" you want to be, and what it is you want to achieve in a specific domain.

Always compare your efforts with what seems critically favored at the time; what claims are made for its privileged status.

Distinguish yourself from the crowd. The best

bit of criticism I ever got was that some early mixed-media collages I'd shown were nice and attractive, but faded into masses of things that were just like them, what Barthes calls the "studium," or unremarkable class of images and objects.

You have rightly understood the importance of historical awareness. This should not be limited to art objects alone, however, but should include the social, political, and economic circumstances under which their makers have labored. This can be a catalyzing force and provide the foundation for a purposeful mission. For example: As an African American, descended from a people enslaved to serve the interests and benefits of dominant "Whites," I am acutely aware of the weakness of my position within the wider world, and even more so in the institutional structure of the art world. We were not present at the creation. Black people were no more involved in the codification of "Art World" terms than we were signatories to the treaty of Versailles, when Western powers and Russia further carved up Africa into their provinces of influence. As late-comers, we do not yet control enough independent institutions, nor the capital resources to mount a competitive challenge to the "mainstream." Outsiders can take nothing for granted in such a subjective field.

If you are Black, you really are coming from behind.

As the Japanese asserted, *oitsuke*, closing the distance, and *oikose*, overtaking white folks, thereby weakening white dominance, is the challenge we face. It took a while, but I finally realized we are not all in this race together. If your recognition depends on the kindness and generosity of others, you are in a world of trouble, buddy. There's a competition going on. The art world is not a level playing field. If you're going to play, though, you've got to play for keeps, and play to win.

An artist is a business professional like any other. It takes tremendous resources and a good accountant to maintain a practice long enough to evolve and stabilize. Only longevity allows a truly meaningful, and realistic, assessment of one's achievement.

There are no workable timetables for career success, so take your time. The urgency that drives you, that propels you into the studio every day, should be the desire to see figures as yet unrealized. If this is where your heart is, integrity will not be an issue.

Sincerely,

Kerry James Marshall
Chicago

Dear Young Artist,

New York is a tough city. It is complex and beautiful. Cities are amazing and brutal. We love cities. They survive, we survive. Each individual finds a way alone or with the help of others.

One must know when deciding to become an artist – it is an irresistible attraction – that there are no guarantees of success, rewards, recognition, etc. One chooses or is drawn to a life of producing works that have no practical use in a largely indifferent world. The way is not easy or comfortable. To be an artist you must love art – and you must respect and find a haven for yourself in your work. It is important in life to find a basic pleasure – intellectual, sensual, kinetic, touch, smell, sight . . . "the shape, the sense, the feel of things" (Hilda Doolittle). Life in general is a miraculous phenomenon full of contradiction for all.

To be in a city like New York or Los Angeles or Mexico City is to be in a dialogue with a community of people that inspire and inform one another.

One should understand fear – fear of failure, fear of not getting this or that. Fear is a device to control us, to stop us in our tracks, to keep us from questioning the erosion of basic human rights. It is the tool of the oppressor. Fear can be a warning. Sometimes I go toward fear, and it is a veil. What are you afraid of?

When I began to produce work for a public in

1968, I was 32. It was the right time and place. In working with concepts of performance and video, I imagined that I was exploring new territory. It was a time of change – of crossing boundaries, breaking forms, merging, turning upside down and backward, of dialogue with artists, musicians, dancers, filmmakers . . . it was fantastic. The work was important.

Now is fantastic. Art is communication, and one must share, show, learn about others, exchange, but not necessarily in a commercial gallery. Decades ago, a center shifted from Paris to New York, but now there is no center. You don't have to be in New York, nor is it necessary to rush from the precarious state of becoming into the marketplace. People seem to rush from here to there for no reason without thinking. You have to find time for yourself. To take chances. Art is not safe. It is a gamble – it can be dangerous. Safe imagination can be boring.

I can see interesting work, beautiful work, but often it seems to be too much looking back at itself, playing it safe, repeating old gestures. True for old artists as well. (young inside always)

Thank you for your letter, Young Artist. Maybe someday we will meet.

The answer is the Work. To Work. To care about the Work.

Sincerely,

Joan Jonas
New York

PS: Be careful not to be overwhelmed by unimportant details. Schedule time every day for your work. There are many examples of poets, for instance, who were doctors, worked in insurance companies, or banks. Find a way to support yourself that is not a compromise. Years ago I saw a photograph in a Canadian magazine of an old woman sitting on the ground surrounded by wooden objects she had made. She was outside the system you refer to. She was smiling and it seemed that she loved her work. For me, this was inspiring.

Dear Young Artist,

Yes, I think you can do both, participate in the art world and maintain your integrity. But your success in doing it depends on your relationship to your art.

I've been teaching at Bard College for more than twenty years. I've also had the opportunity to meet graduate students at several institutions over the years. More and more, I see students who are driven by a desire to have a show in Chelsea and be a successful artist. Certainly not all students, but I've seen a definite shift.

This is understandable, of course. However, for me, it has little to do with why I make art. I believe that art is made to explore the world and the culture, to explore the chosen medium, to explore one's self. It is made to communicate, in the medium's language, a perception, an observation, an understanding, an emotional or mental state. It is made to answer, or try to answer, questions. It is made for fun. In short, it is made in response to personal needs and demands.

A student might see a great work of art and say to himself, "This is a great work of art. I want to make a great work of art, too." And so, the student sets out to try to do so. And if he has some talent, he might produce something that looks just as though it were a work of art — almost convincing. If one didn't know any better one might actually mistake it for a work of art. The only problem is that the great work of art that the student so admired was not a product of these same motives. It was the by-product of the artist's personal quest.

Having ambition is not a problem. In fact, ambition is necessary to be able to carve out the time needed to produce your work from the multitude of other demands on your life. The question is how that ambition is directed. If you adhere to your personal path, having shows and sales will not do any harm. In fact, you might actually make enough money to live, even live well. There's nothing at all wrong with that. The problem comes when the market begins to influence your motives and decisions. If your work needs to evolve and change, it may mean abandoning an approach that brought you recognition.

Of course, you do want to establish your voice as an artist and to, as you put it, "develop a true sense of self." But if you wait until you know you've finally found it, you may never have a show. Finding your voice may be a process, not a goal. I have students who start studying photography in college and tell me that they want to "express themselves." I think to myself, "You're only eighteen, how can you express yourself when you don't know yourself?" But that shouldn't deter them. In learning and practicing an art, they may embark on the path of finding themselves.

I have one final thought to add. In doing so, I may be misjudging you and doing you a disservice. But I sense from the tone of your letter that you may be using your moral dilemma as an excuse for not engaging in your work and that you are using your vulnerability to deflect criticism from me. Cut it out!

Good luck and best wishes,

Stephen Shore
Tivoli, New York

Dear Young Artist,

I started my career as a young artist in 1957. Then, there was not the money in art that there is today. Therefore, one made art because one needed to do so. I taught public school five days a week and painted when I could. I got married and participated in having two children, which made it more difficult to make art. I lived in National City, California, not an art center.

My advice? Don't go into art for fame or fortune. Do it because you cannot *not* do it. Being an artist is a combination of talent and obsession. Live in New York, LA, Köln, or London. As for money: If you're talented and obsessed, you'll find a solution.

Yrs in art,

John Baldessari
Venice, California

Dear Young Artist:

You misjudge me if you think I am someone who has "maintained integrity and freedom of thought *and* participated in the art world" successfully. Although the art world has acknowledged and supported me indirectly over the years, I do not consider myself a gallery artist in so far as, with one exception, I have not made graphic or media work that is designed for gallery spaces. The one solo exhibition that appears on my résumé was composed primarily of dance photos and memorabilia, and was conceived by a curator, not by me.

My career was launched not in the art world as such, but in a community of dancers, composers, and artists who could afford not to be concerned about their careers at a time when this was possible. The economics of living in New York, for one thing, allowed us to immerse ourselves in ideas rather than real estate, and to have low or no expectations of making a living at what we did. Success was measured not by the number of shows we were invited to be in but by the respect of our peers. Again, perhaps, the result of economics. A friend of mine paid $19 a month for an apartment (I paid $45), and no one questioned one another's monetary resources. Furthermore, the pressure that comes from making a salable object that can be inserted into the market economy was entirely lacking in the production of dances. This was one more factor that allowed us to work unfettered by – and happily oblivious to – the potential for monetary rewards.

I must admit that the "good old days" I parade before you lasted only a few years, from around 1960 to 1964, after which a general diaspora took place – both geographically and professionally – as artists found galleries and teaching jobs and choreographers began to institutionalize themselves with companies and boards of directors. Which seems to be the usual route of avant-garde movements. Far from judging such developments, I only wish to emphasize, with the utmost fervor, how important it is for a young artist to delay "professionalism" as long as possible. Find some way to give yourself a chance – and time – to experiment, take risks, play, fool around, even fail, before trying to launch a career. Show your work only to a few devoted friends. Art schools should be a congenial site for this kind of engagement, and sometimes they are. But, as I have frequently found, art schools also tend to serve as launching pads for careers by fostering the same emphasis on polish and completion that one finds in the art world. Challenge yourself with what "doesn't work." Know your sources and what influences show up in your work. Don't worry about originality, but be self-critical, and find ways to accept and deliver supportive criticism among your peers. Don't get hung up on creature com-

' can come later. Try to see every-

t I can observe of younger artists

today, those who are most positive about the state of the art world have banded together to form their own cooperatives, for exhibitions as well as living and working arrangements. You need one another as never before.

Best of luck,

Yvonne Rainer
New York

Dear Young Artist,

Nice to hear from you. While I have some skepticism about your questions and the commonplaces that lurk behind them, I am happy that you are writing to me and hopefully I can give you some guidance you will find worthwhile. Schools are worthless for this kind of information, and every real artist eventually goes to others to learn from their lived experiences what it is one can expect to encounter in one's own career. I survived as a young artist and my work grew because of the kindness and support of older artists. I owe them everything and that is a debt that gets repaid this way.

But that's a mixed blessing, isn't it? Another part of me wants to ask if you are kidding. Isn't the voice of geezerdom, with its war stories and self-regard, the last thing a young artist wants to hear? Who can stand one more story about My First Loft in SoHo, you know, the one that rented for $100 a month? Or how about The Day I Met Duchamp, How I Stretch My Canvases, The Beautiful Blonde on the Train to Paris? Isn't it high time the old folks shuffled off and room was made for the new ideas and language of the young? What can I possibly say that might be of interest to a cool kid like you? My generation, well, we are just in your way – and we know it, too. The reality, as usual, is all mixed up. It is good to be reminded of the commonalities of our experience, that we have brothers and sisters – even parents and children

— and that we are not alone; still, it's a bore to be buttonholed by some garrulous old uncle who really just wants to brag about his own successes.

But heart speaks to heart — and I *do* want to talk to you. Edward Dahlberg says it is presumptuous to assume we can do anything to help another person and it is vulgar not to try. Maybe if I keep it short and sweet and touch on a few obvious points we'll both get out of these letters with our spirits intact.

First of all, welcome to New York City! It's a trip, isn't it? More art, more artists, more art noise than anyplace on Earth. Ever. You ask about the necessity of New York and, no, it's not *really* necessary but it is so unique and so intense that it's worth some degree of sacrifice and discomfort to play this game. If you can find a way to live and work in New York you would be mad not to. If you can't find a way, well, then there are all those Urbinos to our Florence, like Berlin or Los Angeles — hell, LA is probably a Venice! — or lots of other interesting places. But I would hope that every young artist tries this energy hit on for size, to establish a standard of the art life that the rest can be measured against. Charles Burchfield, Myron Stout, and David Smith's careers would suggest to me that the only important location is the studio. And how often did Matisse actually get to Paris?

You worry too much about the dangers of premature success and recognition. We are all different and not every artist has to work her way through years of apprenticeship and practice before she is somehow ready for the world. Hey, we artists have it tough enough that I would never suggest that there is any good to be found in avoiding early success and whatever confrontation with capitalism that might entail. We each make this call for ourselves. Masaccio and Eva Hesse, to name two, seem to have survived their early laurels. Believe me, the preservation of virtue requires a lot more effort than simply ducking a creepy art dealer or some fawning journalist! Integrity, like freedom, is an earned condition and you must find it, in any milieu, for yourself. The worst thing about being embraced young might be the implication that one's work can be easily understood. I think of Jean-Luc Godard sneering at Roger Vadim that he was "only on time." Now *there's* a curse that artists can understand.

For myself I prefer careers that last thirty years to those that last thirty months, but there is no reason to believe there is always more integrity to one pattern than the other. Let's face it, it's not like this is something that is under our control. Not really. Much of the time, if an artist is any good, she is developing a way of understanding the spirit and the stuff of the world that is bound to go beyond the way just about everyone else sees and thinks about it, at least for a while. We are not ignored for malicious reasons, alas. Recognition, when it comes, sometimes can seem like a misunderstanding. The real life of the artist is solitary.

The central fact of artists' lives – the part that non-artists never seem to quite understand – is the loneliness of the studio. Before our runs are over we will have spent more time – thousands upon thousands of hours – alone, just staring at these things we make. This part of our experience must be factored in to every idea about artists' lives if you want to understand them. More artists stop working because of this loneliness than for any other reason.

If there is one essential survival skill that you must learn, it is how to sustain yourself and your work over the years. There is really only one way to do this, and that is by loving what you do, being fascinated by your work, and by being obsessed with making art. You will get in trouble if you need the approval of others to keep your work moving forward. After all these years, the one essential element in my practice, the one thing I am sure of is that I need to be interested in and happy about what I am doing in the studio.

So many of the concerns you bring up in your letter, these worries of yours – the Seduction of Commerce, the Cost of Studio Space, the Need to Develop a Sense of Self – they all sound like the topics for think pieces in the *Sunday Times*, and they have the same slightly banal gravitas. ... atter fish to fry, you and I, some ... portant issues to ponder, like the mys- ... space and light and color and form.

The rest is just living, and your problems there, my friend, are the same as everyone else's. There's nothing special about the *world* part of the *art world* although we like to pretend there is.

Let's get back to work.

Thomas Nozkowski
High Falls, New York

Dear Y.A.,

May this note find you well. Thank you for yours, and for asking a good question.

How to maintain one's integrity and freedom of thought . . . there is a more serious question inside that question: How do we make art that contributes to humanity's common intellectuality?

Money, in its aspects of "fame and fortune," especially in the United States with its culture of commerce, has told everyone that it is the standard of success. (Or, as Bob Dylan said, "Suck Cess.") Money never stops jabbering, but that does not mean we must listen all the time.

It is money that makes you ask about integrity. Don't ask me, but ask yourself: "How can I join the world I live in?" "How can I speak with people who are smarter than me?" (Those people can be anywhere, on any street-corner.)

Imagine if we were writers. Distribution, the publishing world, is valuable to us. But the real importance lies in the question, "How can I write in ways that contribute?"

Everything else follows.

Good luck to us,

Jimmie Durham

Berlin

Dear Young Artist:

We're guessing you're a woman, since the majority of art students have been female for decades. Get ready to work harder and for fewer rewards than the guys next to you. If you're an artist of color, multiply those difficulties.

We're not going to advise you about your work, that's for you to figure out. Instead, we want to talk about why you should be an activist as well as an artist, and how you can find your own unique, outrageous way to fight injustice, like we did.

We put up our first GG posters in the streets in 1985. We were looking for a place to put our frustration, but we also wanted to have some fun criticizing an art system that was so unfair. We never thought we'd still be at it in 2006! The overwhelming public response to our GG work has empowered us in our lives as activists and in our real lives as artists, too. Some of us want – and have – a piece of the pie, while others would like to blow the whole pie up and start over.

Sure, the art world's better now than ever before, especially at the entry level where everyone wants to see what women and artists of color have to say. But galleries still overwhelmingly show white males, and up the ladder, at the level of museums, auctions, and art history books, there's a crushing glass ceiling, way worse than in a lot of other fields.

Let's face it, it's hard for anyone to succeed

at making art, especially in a system that manufactures scarcity, then sells it for big bucks to rich collectors. Museums suck up to these art investors, ask them to sit on their boards and let them decide what to save for the future. We think that's a lousy way to preserve our culture!

So you need to make sure your work endures. Whether you do that as an art world insider or outsider, you'll have to spend some time away from your work, out of your studio, communicating and engaging with whatever art world you decide to live in. Be aware of the system. Don't be afraid to stand up and criticize it. Be inventive. Do some creative complaining! Calculate, embarrass, humiliate, when necessary. Make 'em laugh at themselves and maybe, just maybe, you can get the powers-that-be to move, if only a few centimeters. And don't forget to have fun doing it! That's the very best part!

Some ideas:
Measure the diversity of artists in shows. Then sticker the information in important places, like inside the toilet stalls of major museums and galleries! We did a recent count at the Met in New York. The figures were pathetic: Only 7 percent of the work on exhibit was by women. We put that stat on an artwork we did for the Venice Biennale!

Be a Secret Santa: Each holiday season, deluge curators, critics, textbook authors, and collectors with e-mails asking if they've been naughty or nice to women and artists of color.

Organize postcard campaigns to egregious offenders. Organize counter events to publicize the issue. We deluged the Guggenheim with mail about an all-white, all-male show opening in SoHo. Then, a woman was quietly added to the show! We had our own opening party outside with hundreds of supporters and our own band!

Dress up and organize your own docent tours of galleries and museums. Explain the art world Olympics: how choosing a few artists to win everything makes the visual arts an expensive, precious commodity that only millionaires can afford! Imagine if art was cheap and available to everyone.

Put postcards of your and your friends' work in the postcard racks of museum bookshops. List this intervention on your résumé as your first museum exhibition.

Think of yourself as the Permanent Resistance. Imagine a better system for making, showing and collecting art. Then work to make it a reality! We've been doing it for years. Help us finish the job.

Things don't change without activism. (Ars longa, but so is activism.)

Go Ape with us,

Frida Kahlo and Kathe Kollwitz, Guerrilla Girls
New York and Los Angeles

Dear Young Artist,

Painting is a social act and develops out of a community. Find your community.

Trust your intuition and taste. Taste is a moral code.

Understand art that you don't "get."

High art defines what we see. We see culturally. Seeing is a variable determined by that with which we are assaulted. A new vision and a new art should be the aspiration of high art.

Work as hard as you can to develop craft skills.

Read all you can and remember that by the time you've read it a large part of what you read is obsolete.

You have the audience you deserve. To enlarge or improve your audience requires all the energy you have. You get back what you put out.

If you fail, at least you should have learned something.

Good luck.

Sincerely,

Alex Katz
New York

Dear Young Artist:

Perhaps you and your friends are both right. It's not easy to make an assessment without knowing your work. I'd say the most important thing is to grasp the quality of your own work before worrying about other things. I've lived in China, Japan, and the United States and had to start over twice as a young artist and once as a somewhat older artist.

In China, I worked as a stage designer for a theater troupe to support my life as an artist. I forged receipts so that I could get reimbursed by my employer for my own painting materials. When I left for Japan, I brought my paintings with me, which were works that took much exploration. On the one hand, I was determined to stop taking part-time jobs in order to support my art; on the other hand, I could not bear selling my precious paintings for a cheap price. Therefore, I painted popular Chinese landscapes to sell to Japanese collectors who love Chinese culture. These sold for little money, anywhere from $50 to a few hundred dollars. Later on, some of these paintings fetched a few thousand dollars. Concurrently, I continued doing what I considered as my "real" work. People who were involved in contemporary art that saw this work and recognized its value encouraged me to keep on creating. I was fortunate that my work received attention and was exposed to a broader audience.

Whether you are working in a restaurant, washing dishes, painting portraits on the street for money, or showing in some gallery in order to sell is not so important. These are means to make a living. As long as you have a goal and find a path to reach this goal artistically while maintaining your creative power, and do not lose confidence along the way – these are the real points. But perhaps making a living with paintings keeps you closer to your materials and aspirations.

My third move was from Japan to the United States I was quite well known in Japan by then but I wanted more of a challenge because I felt that my artistic foundation was especially thin. With an Asian Cultural Council grant, I went to P.S.1 International Studio Program in New York. I had to start again. In order to calm my anxiety about my financial burden and desire to succeed, I painted a series of Guanyin oil paintings. This not only occupied my time and kept my hands in paint, but also gave me shows in Japan, which brought an income for my first years in the United States. At the same time, I traveled around the country, visited museums, and did a series of small explosion works, which later became known as *The Century with Mushroom Clouds – Projects for the Twentieth Century*. With the groundwork laid in China and Japan, I established myself quickly in the United States from there.

Regarding your question of artistic integrity and commercial interest, they are not always in conflict with each other, though they can be. It is, in fact, a challenge for me still not to be led and confused by commercial ambition; more prominent artists and masters are also plagued with the question. But one's ability to survive will instinctively arise, and survival requires creativity.

I hope this is of help to you, as I hastily write these words on a plane back to New York. Without seeing your work it is hard to be more specific. Perhaps we can meet if time allows?

Yours,

Cai Guo-Qiang
New York

Dear Young Artist,

Your questions are confusing to me. Looking back, I don't remember asking any of them of myself. Armed with a ridiculous amount of confidence and an inflated sense of the importance of my work, I simply set about it. I went to art school and then moved to New York. I was fearful and panicked setting out on my own, but I did it anyway.

One of the first things I learned after moving to New York is that no one can make decisions for you or tell you what you should do. There are no right answers. I have made sure to work with people that I trust and enjoy. I like showing my work; it is a privilege that feeds the work. And I am very careful to preserve time in my studio, to not overextend myself.

In art and in life all of our actions are at once inextricably bound to circumstance and filled with choices we make from a vast and unlimited array of what's possible. The dance between the two poles of circumstance and unlimited possibility is what generates meaning and passion. I would advise you not to believe for a moment the vein of art criticism and theory that natters on incessantly about the emptiness and failure of the avant-garde. You are a person, armed with free will and the tools to discover that will. You can make things that embody your sense of what matters. You can have conviction, passion, and belief. That there are many forces out there intersecting your work is exciting, challenging, and invigorating. Commerce has always been part of human relations and public life. It is one system of communication among many.

Love,

Jessica Stockholder
New Haven, Connecticut

Dear Young Artist,

I received your letter and felt sad that it is so very hard now for the young artist in New York. It is also difficult for the older artists who, although they started at an easier time, are struggling with the usual enormous expense of living in New York, and additionally face all the problems of aging and having elderly family to support as well. I think New York is always a problem unless you are a billionaire. I feel you are correct in seeing as much art as you can, as well as meeting other artists and sharing your experiences.

One thing I would warn you about: Be careful of whom you let into your studio. I remember two artists who lived near each other and often visited each other's studio. One had an earlier and better chance to show than the other and took her friend's idea and showed it first. So you need to be very self-protective and shrewd.

Also, as best as you can, be aware of the art world's foibles and how it is constructed. Try to get a sense of the galleries, museums, and auction houses as they are very intertwined to the point where one wonders about insider trading among the most elite members of the art world hierarchy. One of the things I did was to use statistics to try to analyze the situation, especially for artists of color (Latino, African American, Asian, Middle Eastern, Native American, etc.). There are of course the usual tokens and collaborators. I wanted the knowledge to understand what I was and was not seeing. I did not want to be a "good German," so to speak. I also did a lot of reading and self-searching to try to understand my strong points and my weaknesses. I tried to be aware of other people's behavior and motivation so I would not take it all so personally. My findings were that there was a definite bias throughout the art world against people of color and often women. To this day I am still dealing with this issue and hope that you prefer to become fully aware of some of the underpinnings of the art world. Some prefer to show in this environment, taking advantage of the restricted opportunities to push themselves forward with what is called white privilege.

One of the things that I find very helpful is this: If you open your studio or have a show and you get verbal or published criticism that is not positive, write it down or talk it into a tape. I find that that gets it off my mind, as I do not need to bother remembering it because it is captured along with my reactions to it. Once you have distance from it, you can decide what is useful.

You should also try to be aware of archival practices so that your work will physically survive. Also be sure to keep track of where your work is and who owns it. Records that I kept or did not keep years ago have profound consequences for me now – positive or negative. Try to select your representatives carefully. Do they pay the artist, and how quickly, when the work is sold? Will they tell you who bought it and for how much? Are they truly honest? One big caution is showing abroad, as there can be economic losses. One can have problems with import and export tariffs and taxes on art that vary from country to country, as well as large shipping bills. The best way is to have a reliable dealer take on that headache for you if you can trust her.

We all isolate ourselves. Try to get together with people you trust. Also keep your mind fresh. I try to read every day from about 11:00 P.M. until 1:00 or 2:00 A.M., or I try to read first thing in the morning. The hard part is finding enough work (a job) to pay the bills — and pay off student loans — so that you can afford to make art. I worked for a museum for twelve years (five days a week or more) before I could find a teaching job. Some artists work in construction, some work on Wall Street, some wait tables or work for other artists. Some teach and some are librarians. Whatever works for you. Try not to get overly discouraged. Isolation can also cause this. One thing that helps is reading about the lives of other artists.

I wish you all the best. Be true to your work and try not to take the pits and valleys of the art world personally.

Howardena Pindell
New York

Dear Young Artist,

Being an artist is one of the coolest things in the world – potentially and actually. Having bright visions of what you might do and become – like the sublime mountain of your career – are critical and motion making. You become what you visualize, and your art becomes what you visualize it to be. Yes, it's possible to show and be public and also follow your own certain way. In fact, you can't be completely alive unless you're conversing with the world. Yup, you might be holding back too much, but imagine the gallery you'd feel best showing in. (Only a few will feel close to right.) Sometimes thoughtless action is the best. Well, not quite thoughtless, but somewhat devil-may-care, I'm-going-to-run-like-hell-with-the-ball.

Which you invented, the "ball" being your ideas and visions that come out of your own nowhere. Don't get too historical a perspective, I'd say, or you might get too close to thinking you're history making art instead of you making it. However, look out: On a level, you're humankind itself, standing on all its past and possibility, making art – further forming mankind. But don't forget individuality. The personal and the universal. Both are important, and tricky to keep juggled right in the formula.

Your intuition can steer you through. Working in the world? Well, you straddle two worlds, inner and outer – source and stage. Keep the art coming from the source, and get it to the stage.

You just got out of art school; you're ambitious – hey, you moved to New York; that's aggressive; continue it; think up work and show in galleries and try to gol-dang say what you think and feel in the world! in such a way that the world stands to have more fun and get better, and you too.

OK, I've said it. A value. The only art worth doing is the art that makes things better. More actually advanced. More enjoyable. A key: genuine happiness. All around.

So, make art that comes out of your own sense of what's actually best, and advanced, and supercool. Do you live on a planet, or on a multi-blither of unknown galaxies?

Best regards,

John McCracken
Los Angeles

**DeaR 'Young' Artist,

My grAndmother told me I wAs going to be An Artist befoRe I knew what An Artist was. She toook me to see JAcob LAWWWW—RencE ^and Mel EdwARds and Bette SaaR^ At the WhitnEy MuSEUM of (AmeRicaN) ARt and heR own WORK At the Studio MuseuM of HaRleM. To be cleAR: my grAndmothER WAS not A pRofessional ARtist, shE cleaned houSES « » to MAKe A living. In fact that'S how shE got this ideA thAt I could be AN ARtist. see Some of heR clients weRe ARtists. To MAke A long stoRy shoRt, shE cooked up this ideA I could meet these Artists if I helped hER cleAn theiR houses. « » My grANDmothER felt meeting these ARtists, real ARtists who ACtually MAde A living making ARt, would help me in some wAy. « » Both of the ARtists (she introduced me to) weRe white, jewish ANd in theiR 60's oR 70's. (Both weRe ModeRnist but not too ModeRnist, just enough.) Both hAd been in thE camps duRing WoRld WAR II. I sAw theiR « » nuMbeR tAttoos. Both weRe VERy humble And self-effAcing About being ARtists. Both WORKed VERy hard ANd WERE not…SupER Rich…ZZZZZZZZ***….

I Am not suRe what I leaRned ^Right thEn And thERE^ About being A (successful) aRtist. FOR A long…time I thought you hAd to be old « » experienced « » ANd « » somehow eaRNed it….?...I wAs 12 whEN this happened. 7 yeARs lateR ^I leaRNEd^ that veRy young Artists* could be good successfu&$ ARtists. But I still thought this WAS AN Anomaly. It seemed to me thAt most folks would have to do some other lAbor to suppoRt themselves if thEy chosE to be ARtists. This MAde sense to me. It still does. So Enjoy yoUR hateful dAy job. It is probAbly giving you ^much^ moRe thAn youR dReAmed of gAllery will eveR pRovide. And if you « » eveR « » get A gAllery, don't come Running to me wheN thEy cheat you oR make you feel like cRAp. We ^ARtists^ desErve the ArtWORld we create. As foR ^being^ A blAck ARtist, which I claiM to be, I think it's ^About^ gtwo things PROFOUUND simultaneous: A...love...of duchaMpiaN pRopoRtions And A struggle only Hannibal, nAy only his elephants could enDUure But foR me it is Achoice « » ^thAt^ is kno eAsy to make, ^ANd^ it is not a cetRain choice .... it is A beautiful trubling choice that seems choice-less on the won hand and on the otheR An infinity of possibilities swiRling—I met a young blAck womaN who thought I wAs being irresponsible in the Articulation of blackness in my work (hmmmmmmm)—if I WAS——tttwo be responsible////who's responsibility would I model my nEW won responsibility on? Hers? AAAss-tAchment to family, tribe, chuRch, The STATE even one's %%rt gallery can be goo?????—but attachment is A hindrAnce if it requires...........thAt you leave youR cRiticality**** behiNd——————

Love WPL
Lewiston, Maine

*eg. jAsper johns, 25 yRs. Old And a communist,

no–solo show aAt MOMA
**dear = beloved
***= I just fell asleep
****=substitute criticality for ass alternately back and forth like a yo-yo or dr. Jekyll and his mother or the blinking lights of a motel sign

Dear Young Artist,

I, as you, have put off writing to you, because I am not seeing you in person to gauge your responses to what I say. Would you blink, blinking back some fear or embarrassment you might not want to expose, if I say this or that? If I were facing you, I could change my direction, make space more real or possible for you in what I say. In a letter, you are a "Young Artist" in the abstract. I am worrying about your uniqueness, about not honoring your uniqueness. Are your sensibilities rawly close to the surface or protected by a fresh urban armor? Will you have any clue what I am talking about? Can this be a good and helpful thing for you or a stumbling block? But we're stuck on paper; so here goes.

I believe that art is the articulation of human freedom. Remember, above all, you are the boss, The Boss, of your freedom. No one else. Your art, if it is original and worth something, expands all human freedom.

Art, after it comes through you, will be different. Art comes from you, you all by yourself, unique among anyone who has ever lived in the history of the world; AND, art comes from you in *your* world with the choices you make as a free being, and the glue, even, with the relationships that you create and stick to; AND art comes from you as a citizen *in* the world; AND you *within* history and in nature.

It is your job to re-invent art itself, through what you create.

This is not the job of critics, theorists, and curators. They follow. We lead, shape, and bend the path of history.

I'm not saying throw out history. But the main history we work from is from artist to artist: handed down. Actually, to save your neck, you can learn to talk to artists, even those from hundreds and thousands of years ago: Bring them your problems, your terrors, your dreams, practical things you have to solve.

You don't have to shape up to someone else's definition of "the artist." Make it up, make up the whole thing, while you're doing what you have to do to survive. You are even free to open yourself up to survival and maintenance of your choices as fountains of your art; you can let these tough customers flow through you.

You worry about showing too early. I disagree. Because you will change, become a new person, many many times over through the years. You will re-invent yourself out of your circumstances and your will. If you show later, you're someone else. Showing can keep a kind of integrity to who you are at the moment.

I used to worry about that when I was young. I actually thought I would keep silent for ten years before I opened my mouth about anything. Now I think that's ridiculous. I was a certain kind of spirit then, and a different one ten years later. Shmushing your young spirit into a more "mature" spirit is being violent to oneself as one is through time.

You ask about the art world and worry about it

corrupting you. First of all, you only mention galleries in relation to the art world. You don't mention the streets, the water, the air, the land, below the land. You don't mention cities, urbanism. You don't mention outer space, inner space, multiple scales, microscopic scales. WHAT? You don't mention the public domain, democracy, the meaning of *public*.

You don't mention the people who receive or who could enter into direct relationship, even interactive relationship, with your art.

You don't mention changing the world itself, bursting all categories, starting over, re-inventing everything. WHAT?

You can see here that I come from the 1960s and 70s. It's so obvious.

So I think the "Art World" is a much more huge entity than you mention. It's way bigger than galleries.

BUT, I cherish the art world. The whole art world. It can be cruel, cold, indifferent; but it is also a world that you can shape. That's where there are people who can listen to you at the deepest level, more than anyone. People who can come across you – even people that you may never meet – and who will make it possible for you to keep believing in your own struggle, even if you become desperate. They are at the essence of the enterprise of making and continuing to make until you have no more breath to breathe! It is the art world that has kept art going from eons ago, responsible to art as if it were one's own child.

So I wish you a long life and great courage. Believe in yourself and work your ass off.

Mierle Laderman Ukeles
New York

IN RESPONSE TO A FELLOW ARTIST:

ART IS MADE FROM THE NECESSITIES OF A HUMAN BEING NOT CONTENT WITH THE CONFIGURATION AS IT IS PRESENTED TO THEM. IF ART REMAINS A QUESTION THERE IS NO DIFFICULTY IN MAINTAINING ONE'S INTEGRITY & FREEDOM OF THOUGHT WITHIN A PUBLIC CONVERSATION.

(ALL PARTICIPATIONS IN EXHIBITIONS & PRESENTATIONS OF WORK IN ANY MANNER OR FORM ARE IN FACT CONVERSATIONS WITH YOUR OWN TIMES.)

THE QUESTIONS OF MAKING A LIVING ARE THE SAME EXISTENTIAL QUESTIONS ALL MEMBERS OF A SOCIETY HAVE. THE ADVANTAGE OF THE ARTIST IS THAT THE USE OF THEIR PRODUCT IS NOT DEPENDENT UPON BEING IN ACCORD WITH THE POWERS THAT BE!

AS TO RIGHTNESS OR WRONGNESS: THESE ARE THINGS THAT CAN ONLY BE DETERMINED WITHIN A PUBLIC SPHERE.

IF YOU FEEL YOU HAVE WHAT TO SAY, YOU ARE BEHOLDEN TO FIND WHERE TO SAY IT.

ART IS NOT ABOUT MAKING SENSE BUT OF DETERMINING MEANING.

BON CHANCE & GIVING THE DEVIL ITS DUE. I LOOK FORWARD TO SEEING YOUR WORK IN CONTEXT.

YOURS IN ART,
LAWRENCE WEINER
NEW YORK

To a Young Artist,

You could be 18, 30 or 50, you are young to have decided to be an artist at this time in your life. First let me congratulate you on your choice. From here on, you enter the endless magic life of being an artist.

The world is your oyster: It will provide you with unlimited material for your art. Look at it again from that point of view. Suddenly the world is a different place, so interesting, so beautiful, and so mysterious. Have fun with it. And share your fun with us.

You, as an artist, will unfold the infinite mystery of life and share it with the world. It may just be two people your work will communicate to. Don't be upset. Be upset if you are not happy with your work. Never be upset about how many people have seen it, or how many reviews it has received. Your work will exist and keep influencing the world. Moreover, your work will keep changing the very configuration of our world no matter what kind of attention it gets or doesn't get. So even when you are an unknown artist, be caring of what you make and what you give out. Your work, no matter what, affects the world, and in return, it brings back 10 times what you've given out. If you give out junk, you get back junk. If you give out confusion, you will give yourself confusion. If you give out something beautiful, you will get back 10 times more beauty in your life. That's how it works. You are now like a tree in the park. Your existence is making the city breathe well. So relax and be yourself. Don't try to be anything but yourself. Rely on your instinct and inspiration. Go with it!

By the way, my thanks to you for being an artist. I am aware that I will be one of the many, many people who gets the benefit of your decision. I wish you great success.

I love you!

Yoko Ono
New York

Dear Young Artist,

Thanks for your letter. Yes, it definitely is possible to maintain your integrity and freedom of thought and still participate in the art world. The way to do that is *always* to choose maintaining your integrity and freedom of thought over the art world *whenever* the two conflict. They don't always conflict, so you can have both to some extent. But you won't be able to participate in the art world as fully as possible, unless you're willing to sacrifice your integrity and freedom of thought in order to do so. And you won't be able to maintain your integrity and freedom of thought unless you're willing to sacrifice whatever degree of art world success is necessary in order to do that.

Each time you choose art-world participation over personal integrity when the two conflict, you break more and more of your own spirit – that part of yourself that justifies hope, faith, and trust in others by demonstrating that you are worthy of them yourself. Kill that, and you kill your own self-esteem – that innocent belief in your own goodness that breeds the belief that you deserve the rewards you strive to obtain. Kill that, and you kill everything that gives value and meaning to art world participation, and to the enormous successes and satisfactions it promises. You create for yourself a personal hell of cynicism, suspicion, dishonesty, and self-dislike in all of your relationships that no amount of money, power, or recognition can eradicate (quite the opposite), as well as the noxious, partly buried awareness that you yourself are no better than those you condemn.

On the other hand, choose personal integrity and freedom of thought instead, and you ensure your personal equanimity and contentment no matter how much art world recognition, success, money, or power you must relinquish in order to protect them. Here's why:

Integrity means that you are not tempted to lie to yourself about what you're doing, or why. Your deeply held convictions inform your principles, your principles motivate and guide your actions, and your actions express your convictions. There is an internal coherence – in the best case, harmony – among your beliefs, your emotions, and your actions. This doesn't mean you never experience internal conflict, for example, between the beliefs and the impulse to self-aggrandizement. It means that when you're internally conflicted, you know you are, and know what the issues are, and see the trade-offs clearly. Your self-respect does not depend on rationalizing or making excuses for actions you recognize to be inexcusable; so you're not tempted to debase or misrepresent your core convictions to yourself in the service of getting ahead, and thereby distort your perception of yourself, your options, or their consequences. In order to see clearly when you're tempted to violate your principles, you need a strong sense of self-respect, and – simultaneously – a strong sense of humility. *Self-respect* means you can acknowledge mistakes or flaws without plunging into self-hatred or depression; you can maintain your dignity without deluding yourself that you're perfect. *Humility* means that you can make amends for those mistakes without feeling ashamed; that you can learn from them without losing value in your own eyes. Integrity, inner clarity, self-respect, and humility mutually reinforce one another through the sheer pleasure of heightened self-knowledge, and strengthen the self to withstand threats to its internal unity.

Freedom of thought means that the principles and convictions I've just been talking about spring into your awareness, from a part of yourself that lies beyond the limitations of the individual ego, and that is uncensored by that part of your mind that packages your subjective self-expression for public consumption. It means that your curiosity to know and understand – yourself, your environment, your relationships – is not stifled or constricted by guilt, shame, or fear. Freedom of thought doesn't have much to do with self-assertion, and, even less to do with personal identity or self-indulgence. On the contrary: It is the ability to rise above the narrow constraints of the subjective self, to see and investigate and understand it from a reflective distance, and to be able to use your own personal pet human (i.e., your body) as an instrument for being or doing whatever your principles and convictions tell you is then required – by the circumstances, by your own imperatives, or by intuition. Freedom of thought is inherently connected to the pleasure of self-transcendence, and so to the pleasure of freely acknowledging your own imperfections – with humor, compassion, severity, and accountability.

So integrity *plus* freedom of thought is a powerful and heady combination: It means acting in unity and inner transparency from drives and motives that lie above and beyond the blinkered perspective of the ego, according to uncorrupted principles that you deeply believe in and that inspire your action and clarify your perception, and that are unsullied by fear of public disapproval or ridicule or punishment or retaliation or failure. Integrity plus freedom of thought protects you from this kind of fear because whenever it threatens, you see the trade-off clearly: capitulate and you damage (and eventually lose) the only thing worth aspiring to, the only thing worth having, and the only thing worth experiencing on a moment-to-moment basis as you navigate through your life.

Now about *maintaining* your integrity and freedom of thought. Most of the myriad available spiritual, religious, or psychological disciplines, practiced daily, patiently, stubbornly, over an extended period of time, that put a premium on self-knowledge, self-control, self-discovery, and self-expression as a package can help a lot (if you think I'm talking about navel-gazing, go back and reread the preceding paragraphs). Whatever your discipline is, it has to be a fixed and permanent commitment, a cornerstone of your life that you seek opportunities to practice, without which your day is not complete. Of course this doesn't mean that you practice every day mechanically; exactly the opposite. It means that if you don't practice, you viscerally feel the gradual process of shutting down, becoming numb, mechanical, unreflective, insensitive, sad; of atrophying that part of yourself that gives you reason to live. Once you stop feeling that process, you're lost, and that part of yourself will sink out of reach. So when you fail to practice, thirst for it, grieve its loss, resolve yet again to give it pride of place in your schedule. It doesn't matter whether you always succeed in this resolve. What's important is making that resolve, each day, with the same determination. The more often you make it, the easier it will get – eventually – to act on it, and the more opportunities to practice you will find. Eventually you will find that every situation you confront, and particularly those in which you are forced to choose between personal integrity and art world success, there is an opportunity to practice. And eventually you will greet such choices joyfully, as a chance to celebrate and honor the deep convictions and principles that by now structure, govern, and permeate your self, your awareness, and your experience at all levels. This is the point at which the choice between personal integrity and art world success is so easy as to be no real choice at all.

Young artist, it is highly unlikely that you

will be rewarded professionally for reaching this point. Nor will it make you popular. On the contrary: You will develop a reputation for being "difficult," "uncooperative," "inflexible," or even "self-destructive;" and treated (or mis-treated, ostracized, or blacklisted) accordingly. If these reactions concern you, remember you always have alternatives: to maintain your integrity and accept the rewards, or fall into line and capitulate – and accept the "rewards."

Good luck!

Best regards,

Adrian Piper
Cape Cod, Massachusetts

PS: As for showing early, I don't think you can formulate a hard and fast rule about that. There are important lessons to be learned either way. I started showing internationally before I graduated from art school, and learned a lot from that. I think that just as it's better to live with someone for a while before marrying them, it's better to find out sooner rather than later what the art world is like, so you can decide whether or not it's your lifetime cup of tea.

Dear Young Artist:

Art world participation could spoil your "integrity" and "freedom of thought"? You talk tosh. Only you – on your own – can do that.

Furthermore, anyone employing the word "tainted" in regard to the art world should either grow up or else content themselves with amateur productions. If you intend to make work that you want others to enjoy or appreciate, the [commercial] art world will be part and parcel of your universe: The best art must always be grounded in its contemporary reality, both in its production and in its distribution. Ivory towers are only for the very young, the menopausal of both sexes, or the dissatisfied or disgruntled. The best art seldom resides there.

Lots of gallery opportunities exist for young artists because their work is cheap and thus easy to invest in. If a good gallery is interested in you early on, the only real reason to shy away from showing is the risk that early successes might box you into continuing a praxis that works (i.e., sells), which could then be parlayed into teaching positions, etc., restricting further developments of your work (if you let it). But there's nothing wrong with any of this: It's a pattern common to the greater part of the artists' world.

On the other hand, time to explore yourself won't get you much farther than what you like and dislike. The best art is not based on self, but rather on what's important to imagine – and how best to cogently articulate this. Then again, if you genuinely want "time to develop a true sense of self," I would suggest you take time off from the art world to travel and work abroad to learn how other people think, or perhaps consider gaining a university education (or both). The art world's not going away. You can always get back to it.

Although my own university schooling preceded my art, I have always valued its imparted sophistications, which were critical later in sizing up and deciding my work's trajectories. Knowing a lot about your world, and how things really work over the long run, is a hell of a lot more useful than keeping up with the galleries.

I wish you good luck illuminating your future career's "sublime and invisible mountain" (a Rilke quote perhaps?).

Sincerely,

(signature blocked out – mass production could prove damaging)

Jo Baer
Amsterdam

Dear Young Artist,

Thank you for your letter, your e-mail messages and fax, and for your indefatigable patience while awaiting my reply.

Like other creative practices, making art is about exploring possibilities. The possibilities of materials, the possibilities of ideas, the possibilities of human relations. The moment you pause and try to sort it out, it can get pretty overwhelming. Two hundred years ago, the poet John Keats faced the same struggle: He was overwhelmed with financial difficulties, and when he looked at the stuff that had been written before him – Shakespeare, Spenser, Milton – he resigned himself to the dispiriting question, "What is there left to do?"

He kept at it. In the space of a couple of years he wrote a half dozen odes that took poetry in a new direction, got a lot of bad press, saw his books remaindered, and died just after turning twenty-five. Plus, the girl he wanted said: *no.*

But the thing is, he found a way.

He called it Negative Capability. Rather than trying to make sense of all the details that comprise the worrisome practice of being an artist, he wholeheartedly – and also whole*head*edly – got lost in the process of writing the best poems he could. In a letter to his brothers, Keats described Negative Capability as a way of being, wherein one "is capable of being in uncertainties, Mysteries, doubts, without any able reaching after fact & reason."

mantras go, "Negative Capability" is a pretty good one.

So my advice, for whatever it's worth, is not to worry too much about those uncertainties, mysteries, and doubts. If making art is hard work – and it is – equally hard is the process of being an artist, of bringing the work to a public. This is where human relations are so important. A lot of the stuff I learned about art and being an artist did not come from visual artists; it came from writers like Keats (in his letters) and composers like Ned Rorem (in his diaries) and outdoorsmen like Ray Bergman (who wrote about fly fishing for trout). So read as much as you can and get into the thick of life whenever you can – learn a foreign language, learn things about other people, go places and do things that have nothing to do with art – because it's the stuff that has nothing to do with art that has everything to do with art.

With best wishes,

Joseph Grigely
New Buffalo, Michigan

The editors would like to thank all of the artists who generously gave their time to this project for the benefit of many others. Working with them was a privilege and a treat. Additional thanks to the following gallery staff members, friends, and artists' assistants who helped with practical matters or translation, among them: Sarah Bacon, Jesse Coffino-Greenberg, Ryan Conrad, Linda Earle, Abigail R. Esman, Bethany Izard, Amanda Keeley, Greg Kucera, Stanislas Lahaut, Andrew Leslie, Doreen Mende, Laura Muggeo, Amy Owen, Hanna Schouwink, Lance Wakeling, Lilly Wei, Miyako Yoshinaga, and the staff at *Art on Paper* magazine. And finally, the editors are grateful to Elisa Leshowitz and DAP/Distributed Art Publishers for their enthusiasm, patience, and support.

LETTERS TO A YOUNG ARTIST

Design: Fabio Cutró, Cutró Design, New York

Project Manager: Shelly Bancroft

Editing: Peter Nesbett, Sarah Andress

ISBN: 0-9773680-0-9

An Art on Paper Book
Published by Darte Publishing LLC,
150 West 28th Street, Suite 504,
New York, NY 10001. (212) 675-1968

Distributed by D.A.P./Distributed Art Publishers,
155 6th Avenue, 2nd Floor, New York, NY 10013.

Printed in Canada.
Second Edition 10 9 8 7 6 5 4 3